SHENANIGANS

Born in 1951 in Wales, Patrick Lodge has both Irish and British citizenship. He is a retired university lecturer and has also taken on academic leadership roles for several institutions. His poetry has been published widely in the UK and internationally, including in *Envoi*, *Ink, Sweat & Tears*, *Mediterranean Poetry*, *Revival*, and *The Stare's Nest*, and has been translated into Vietnamese for *Van Viet*. He was the winner of the 2015 Blackwater International Poetry Competition. His first collection of poetry, *An Anniversary of Flight*, was published in 2013 by Valley Press. He currently lives in North Yorkshire.

by the same author

AN ANNIVERSARY OF FLIGHT

Shenanigans

Patrick Lodge

Valley Press

First published in 2016 by Valley Press
Woodend, The Crescent, Scarborough, YO11 2PW
www.valleypressuk.com

First edition, second printing (May 2017)

ISBN 978-1-908853-70-7
Cat. no. VP0087

Copyright © Patrick Lodge 2016

The right of Patrick Lodge to be identified as the
author of this work has been asserted in accordance with
the Copyright, Designs and Patents Act 1988.

All rights reserved. No part of this publication may be
reproduced, stored in or introduced into a retrieval system,
or transmitted in any form, by any means (electronic,
mechanical, photocopying, recording or otherwise) without
prior written permission from the rights holders.

A CIP record for this book is available from the British Library.

Printed and bound in Great Britain by
ImprintDigital.com, Exeter

www.valleypressuk.com/authors/patricklodge

Contents

Small Landscapes 13
Mauerfall 15
Shenanigans 16
New Year Hikers 17
The Spa Quartet 18
The Bus to Ano Mera 24
Yiannis in His Bar 25
Lindos By Night 26
La Poesia Sul Largo 27
Abandon Ship, Dad! 28
Uncle Ho Remembers 30
Tuol Sleng Genocide Museum, Phnom Penh 32
In Arcadia 33
The Priest on the Lake 34
Lligwy Burial Chamber, Anglesey 36
Portrait of an Unknown Planter, 1725 37
Mary Bateman's Lament 38
Notes from the Beggar's Benison 40
Jorvik Afternoon 41
Her Mother's Fur Coat 42
To Miss Jessica Rowland-Jones 44
Ergo Sum 45
The Stone Pickers 46
The Respectable Working Class 48
St. Christopher House 49
A Scenic Life 50
Vanitas 52
The Immortal Game 54
The Governor's Bath-House, Sydney 57
Café Caryatids 58

The Ladies of Doña Sofia 59
Seamus and Paddy Build a Dam 60
The Prof 62
Kite 64
A Simple Game 65
Sure of Father: VE Day, 2015 66
Alphabet Baby 67
Bartimaeus Sees His Way Clear 68
Trio for Roy 71
C'an Freixa 76

Notes 78

Acknowledgements

Some of these poems have appeared in one form or another in the following publications: *The Stare's Nest*, *Envoi*, *The Interpreter's House*, *Ink, Sweat & Tears*, *The Lake*, *Mediterranean Poetry*, *Staxtes*, *The Disappearing*, *Revival*, *Carillon*, *Blue Max Review*, *The High Window*, *Morning Star*.

'Changing,' 'Lindos By Night' and 'Women in the Whirlpool' appeared as part of the Leads to Leeds project curated by Helen Mort, which also included an earlier version of 'Sure of Father: VE Day, 2015.'

'Uncle Ho Remembers' and 'Tuol Sleng Genocide Museum' were translated into Vietnamese by the poet Hoang Hung and published in *Van Viet*.

'C'An Freixa' was Highly Commended in the Poetry Space Competition 2014 and included in the 2014 anthology, *For Want Of A Better Word* (Poetry Space).

'In Arcadia' was the winner of the 2015 Blackwater International Poetry Competition.

'Mary Bateman's Lament' was long-listed for the York Literature Festival Poetry Competition, 2016.

Thanks go to my publisher, Jamie McGarry and to my editor, Rosa Campbell, with whom it has been a pleasure to work.

Special thanks to my friend and artist, Denise Phelps, for the front and back cover artwork.

For Sam, Sally and Alys
'May you live all the days of your life.'

'I could not bear a life with everything perfect.'

JIMMY SANTIAGO BACA

*'Oh poetry
What are you, poetry?'*

HOANG HUNG

Small Landscapes

Sleet falls in sticks
across Brante field,
sweeping the furrows clean
like a besom working a soul.
Every day the philosopher
at the five-bar gate watches
the black dog labour towards him;
splayed paws levering
up the cinder track,
slow, inevitable,
claiming kinship.

At the field edge agriculture
becomes random.
The dialectic of tractor and earth,
the drilled logic of seed lines,
fray into a scripture of switches:
bittersweet, hip, haw, sloe.
Recusant berries stand out
against winter orthodoxy;
remnants of summer warmings,
they are non-conformists.

The philosopher has squandered much
seeking acquaintance with small
landscapes that promise everything
to those who diligently scrape and sift,
collect fancies like nuggets
from a riverbed, stacking them
carefully to corbel a dry, dark peace.

The dog arrives. The wind
slices across the field like a blade
cutting down paper. Clouds
hardly bothering to clear the hill
unfurl in shrouds over the vale.

There is a limited outlook;
he holds to the selvedge,
pulls up his collar,
shrugs and walks on.

Mauerfall

for Alys Grace

We watch the news from Berlin.
Walls fall in Potsdamer Platz; people
swarm like woodpeckers, chiselling
and drilling, expecting to fly free.

Cement becomes elemental, fleshy;
it dilates and the dispossessed push
through. *Wir sind ein Volk* they sing,
tickled at this old world become new.

You were only a few hours born, laid
like proving dough on my chest;
breathing unhurried, eyes closed
with womb dreams, for once at rest.

Shenanigans

I play the fox; what else do you expect in this
moony garden?

You stand, alone at the window, tall, white
as down,

staring as if I was some will-o'-the-wisp,
a green-eyed seducer

versed with pulpit words. Nightly I come to you
with a sermon of shoes:

brogues, balmorals, wingtips, winkle-pickers
trainers and loafers.

Trophies lifted from careless men, cradled in this
cunning grin,

laid out for review and match. I preach a choice,
silly goose.

Let each man claim his own, tie you tight as a lace.
But don't be deceived

by any glib-tongued spiel. Test the snout, the brush,
the shining pelt of it –

my fox paws are real, make no mistake. The woods
call us: stay wild and free,

put on your dancing shoes, step out, trot a tricksy
measure with me.

New Year Hikers

From a mile high the cloister ruins are
a hand gathering up, shaking out
a shroud of barren fields

where New Year hikers meditate on maps,
floundering in the origami world
unfolding at their boots.

The hills around defy ordnance survey;
they rear and slip as if a serpent
had shed skin, slid on

to bow a slow march over the landscape.
The wind whistles contours,
sings bin-bag shreds

stalled on barbed wire like a choir
of salutary crows. Buttresses
lay shadow fingers

on the hikers standing still as notes
on a stave. Pulling up hoods,
they process downhill;

each sole-print in the snow only a guess
as to when they might arrive at the land
that loves silence,

all folds and dints, winter dead.

Fine.

The Spa Quartet

1: Changing

Turner had to imagine
a language to capture it.
This bowl of smoke,
presented in the palms
of the hills, as a midwife
offers up the newly born:
Leeds, 1816,
the first industrial city.

In the spa changing rooms
that's all history.
More scrubbed clean
financial services now,
as the wool blend suits are shed,
the shorts, the washed out Ts,
the branded trainers go on.

But just before
they pitch muscle against treadmill,
three men talk
of last night's football.
In that flat sheen of accent,
there is tappet – a clack
of machinery, in the shuttling
interplay the quick milled asides
that leave a swarf of consonants.
They shim past me,
an exaggerated stiff-legged,
big-balled strut to the machines.

That watercolour city
of loom and scutch,
bobbin and boiler,
still sings loud –
like tectonic plates,
subterranean, dangerous,
making waves.

2: Women in the Whirlpool

Like terrycloth penguins they waddle poolside.
Six women relaxing on a "girl's night in";
slicked back, DIY-facelift ponytails glinting

in the spotlights like oiled feathers.
Wary of predators, scary in their dedication
to fun, they claim a clearing in the forest

of loungers, tables, chairs; form a magic
circle whose incantations are gelish, shellac,
fake bakes, waxes, tatts and goss.

In the whirlpool bath they preen in a lily pad
scurf of declining bubbles; swaying gently
in the flux, transported, as if front row

at a reunion gig for a band from their lost youth.
They chatter in a miasma of celebrity scents,
the clink of Poundland bling. *Oh! It's hot* says one;

Where's the on button? giggles another, bumping
and grinding piercings, inked arse-antlers below
the waterline. They channel distressed mill girls

on Wakes Week, colluding about work, or the lack
of it, complaining about men, or the lack of them;
but when the jets spring up with a bright tiger roar,

the mirror surface dissolves and hard faces,
hard luck follow. Water becomes their element,
softens them. Laid back on green tiles, spinster-

pale arms stretched out, hair loosened, wagged
free, they stare up, vaguely, as nymphs in a forest
pool, waiting, enchanted, for their Hylas to arrive.

3: Swimming Against the Tide

Six old gadgers push off
from the shallow end;
synchronized, line abreast,

arms in slowmo flail,
they breast-stroke forward.
Almost static, suspended -

as pool water, it seems, ebbs
away over speckled shoulders.
Stilled like dogged drumlins,

they hold a pose, as if
uncertain; trout mouths
gasping in a frozen grimace,

a rehearsal for the fishmonger's
marble slab. Heads bob; low sun
glints off swimming goggles,

each rise and fall flashes out
a desperate Morse code,
signalling astonishment

at how far they have swum,
how gutted they are at the deep
end's resolute siren call.

4: Aqua Aerobics

A track-suited attendant leans over,
swabs despondently at the Jacuzzi leak:
I am literally flogging a dead horse.

Metaphorically, I think, looking away
to the pool where the elderly ladies,
waist deep, mitigate gravity

to high volume 60s pop compilations,
bucking and gyring like hippocampi
escaping monsters of the deep.

The tune changes: *March of the Mods*,
with added drum 'n' bass, provokes
a collective tremor of memory. Flotation

devices are held high, at full stretch,
like poles; bright swimsuits stretched tight,
dipped flags of countries that no longer

exist. Above water, all strike heroic poses,
as if Komsomol poster girls at a party rally;
below, hips and knees defy replacement.

The Bus to Ano Mera

Mykonos, 1979

The early morning bus
to Ano Mera stalls
in a whirlpool of goats.
The driver adds his
obscenities to the whistles

bleats and bells
that flow like a fast
current around us.
A woman lifts a child
onto my lap, shifts

two dangling chickens
from right to left,
better to punctuate
her barked invective
with stabbing finger;

her black nails edge
her chopping hand
like a funeral card.
I feel sick you said;
I offered a polo mint.

Yesterday we thought
of death on the plunging
boat to Delos; today,
in this becalmed bus,
we think there may be life.

Yiannis in His Bar

Yiannis in his bar is restless; counting covers,
cradling a cappuccino, he watches

the impossibly taut, tanned staff make money
for him in accents from the Steppes.

He stares at a waitress's legs, remembers wild
nights, drinking with cockney spivs,

dancing film-star syrtaki with peroxide women;
flips worry beads like an impatient groom.

Yiannis lights up his one for the night; rests, where
old men have smoothed the pebble seat

shiny as an ossuary. Eclectic House from his bar,
soundtracks the mute satellite football;

Yiannis conjures the punch of rock 'n' roll, the smell
of patchouli and lust in the backstreets.

Bells toll from the Panagia; incense coils from a censer,
the choir chant the *Kontakion of the Dead*:

Yiannis recalls village girls in their innocence,
forsees his spotless wine-washed bones.

He spits and flicks his butt into the churchyard:
neither sickness, nor sorrow, nor sighing.

Lindos By Night

fishes circle each other in the bay   underwater
a blue and orange child's mobile

hawks hang between beach and citadel   stasis
choreographed   wind chimes on a still day

from the acropolis at dusk the knowing little owl
observes her burnished mirror town

in the tavernas charcoal flares   flesh and herb
smoke rises upwards unsung

with gleaming eyes stoned tourists weave through
painted streets   unwearying

bar televisions flicker silver   reflecting   distorted
Greece   incandescent on city streets

the owl spreads wings but drops too late
to hunt the town for wisdom

La Poesia Sul Largo

(Poetry On The Lake Festival, Orta, 2015)
con grazie a Ernesto Ragazzoni

From the island gate
a serpent rolled out;
its mouth truly
the embouchure,
loose lipping
a stream of words
that hissed
like a silk mist
across the lake,
muffling bells,
swathing all sounds
but themselves.

Words took strength,
became torrents
without inhibition
in this glacial bowl.
Like melt water
they burst through;
floated San Giulio higher,
tongued the Sacro Monte,
caused ferrymen
to focus harder
on the cross-currents.

The serpent inhaled;
rivers, against nature,
returned to headwaters.
The words were read.
The lake subdued.

Abandon Ship, Dad!

"twilight and every bell, and after that the dark"
ALFRED, LORD TENNYSON

Abbadon ship! I could never get the words right.
It would crease you with laughter, literally,
fold you over, a big man bent double, shaking,
tears streaming. You would correct me but

it would start up all over again. Jonah the Jinx,
I think, a buck-toothed sailor making shipmates
abandon ship at first sight. Beano or Dandy?
I can't remember that – just the Saturday morning

house cleaning rituals; the smell of polish, bleach.
We chanted times tables together; I read out loud,
Bash Street Kids, Roger the Dodger. We sang
songs you had marched to; with a mop you showed

parade ground drills; still martial, stiff-backed,
taken back to blanco and bearskins – the rifle mop
slapping hard, affirming, to the floor,
a slippered foot stamping an echo – stand easy!

It stopped being us without me noticing; I stopped
laughing at your jokes so you stopped telling them.
You became part of my peripheral vision but you
kept watch on me, in cuttings, stilted phone calls

visits home, in the grandchildren I once thought
you would have liked to have had first. At the end
it became me watching you, sitting, a premature
revenant, condemned to remorseless self-interrogation,

sniffing, bemused, the ullage of your life as if there was
still a moral to be got that might be passed on, a way
in which this gleed of a life might be flamed again
to illumination. I listened, not as to a conversation,

more as an audience to your monologue; your gift to me,
a miser's hoard of words spent as if you knew already
they were not currency in that place, beyond the tunnel
you stared into, crimped in the chair, like a cox

holding fast to the rudder, calling out, hold water,
hold water… Abandon ship, Dad! Don't cross the bar;
get out of the boat, stay here on this shore with me.
We can still laugh at those comic book heroes;

you and me laughing fit to burst as we buffed and shined.
The tide ebbs, tugs at my ankles in the shallows; bids me
launch. You never had my two penn'orth but I give them
to you now; you are properly buried – let it run easy.

Uncle Ho Remembers

From the Saigon train,
all is earth or water.
Through window grills,
a thin strip of sustenance
shines between sea
and mountain jungle;
rice fields wanton with family tombs
studded across the draught board
of water and berm.
Now the paddy dead
are become ancestors,
germ in the timeless cycle
of seed to spike to seed.

Across the tracks,
light cuts in low
from the tree line;
a cobra flaring,
it recoils from a red-starred obelisk
mooring a uniform
cemetery, a muffled hysteria
of plinths and plaques.
In this lake of abundance
which once snuffed
out the fire at its heart,
which dammed the flood
of bullets and bombs,
Uncle Ho remembers:
his lost family of liberation,
each a grain of gold,

never to ripen. Harvests pass;
nobody comes
to burn joss,
to call their name.

A child on a dyke imitates
his grandfather,
better to become him
when he teaches
his own grandchildren
to follow the buffalo.
He eats fruit, recalls the planting of trees.
In his palm, a bowl of rice,
yellow as a pagoda wall.

Tuol Sleng Genocide Museum, Phnom Penh

You must stare back,
brazenly, stare back.
Widen your eyes
six thousand times:
with these images
seeing is believing.

Look, a child, snapped
with heavy chains
around his neck
as if they feared
he would fly away.

Look, a death pit
dug in a playground;
bone wrists still tied,
skulls blindfolded
as if the dead
might see their killers,
point reproachfully.

Some scowl,
some are wary,
some scared,
some still smile
as if this is a game
whose rules will become clear in time.

Look each person in the eye,
they will not now be discomfited.

In Arcadia

In this tourist town I lie back on a lounger,
embalmed in Factor 50, well-shrouded, white
towelling pulled high over my eyes. I drift between
worlds, like a li-lo in a pool, untethered inside a dome

of sound whose vertices are bird call, wave splash,
chatter…or ice cubes: testing the friction of glass,
they slither and chink, around a circle of lime,
spitted on a cocktail stick. Off to the left or right,

a telephone rings (old style); no-one answers it.
Footsteps tick tock on parquet floor; swell louder
to bring news or fade away in disappointment.
Maybe there is murmuring, where people in stairwells

or cupboards, with an afternoon to fill,
have decided to read lines at each other,
from a play they don't know, could never perform.
In another place there could be dogs sniffing

the air for honey, heads lifted to the river,
expecting to bark – a sharper sound, demanding
respect, as if someone had shouted "clear"
while others stepped back, with rehearsed diligence.

I sit up sharply. The light is failing. The sun sinks
fast here, dropping sheer below the Hotel Sol,
slotting like an obol into an upturned mouth;
still silver-bright enough to shut eyes that stare back.

Touch me…

The Priest on the Lake

Lake Ohrid, 2014

The lake seems hammered flat
to the horizon; a line of silver
solders air to water, each
depthless, opaque to each other.

Two silhouettes, against light
no better than a badly-dipped
candle, like silent movie actors
mime a parody of speed in a water-taxi.

The boatman sits gurning, grits
his teeth, guns the grudging outboard
into a veneer of roar. The keel
chamfers a diamond-bright edge,

true as any orthodoxy, across
the mirror gloss. The priest
in the prow clamps his hat tight,
leaning forward as if fighting a gale

of deviation roaring from all-night
lakeside bars; his beard is a schism,
a paradox split over cassock
and cross. He stares into the lake

seeking resolution in this urgent
dawn journeying, sees nothing
beyond the tain, his reflection
alone against a boundless, blueing sky.

The boatman, more soft-wired,
ductile, looks backwards, smiles
as the scar of wake silently
heals in the salve of shining water.

Lligwy Burial Chamber, Anglesey

I become a worm to myself wriggling
into the lifeless dust under Lligwy.
Squirming to get between stone uprights,
I am eight years old at Saturday confession.
There are the pious, pewed and sacramental,

nervy for queue jumpers, counting off sins
like I count scabs on my knees, waiting a turn
in the gloomy box of ancient air breathed by sinners
who were neighbours, friends, relatives
on the outside. Inside the child, sitting gravely

as the shutters slid back like a boulder being rolled,
talking to a mesh grill so mug-near in the murk
you could smell eternity beyond it. Closer, even,
than the twenty-five tons of megalithic capstone
now propped a few inches from my nose.

Hypnagogic, like Lazarus of the four days,
I hover here between *corpus* and *spiritus*, breath
squeezed shallow by the scarab-backed slab above,
reconciled that all is foretold, enough at least
to forego for now, as then, the release of the shriven.

Portrait of an Unknown Planter, 1725

A trick of the light
or just poor painting,
but from where I sit
the peruked man
seems inside out;
a bone cave of ribs
where lacy coat facings
should be.

He wears his heart
on his sleeve.
He is transparent;
smiles smugly,
one hand opening
his coat, the other
pointing at the great
house on a distant hill.

Such sweet sweetness
is this gentle life.
There is nothing to hide,
he says. *See, deep inside*
there is no blackened soul.

There is no soul.

Mary Bateman's Lament

1: The Prophet Hen

The sun will suck light from your eyes;
the moon will hang bloody in your sky.
Things slip backwards in these dark days;
naught is as it seems, and I, a simple
farmer's daughter, am become midwife
to doomsday. Look, my prophet hen
spells it out clearly – "Christ is coming".
It's a providence: each resurrected egg
a testament to our undeniable fate.
Pay me now; the end times are never late.

2: The Gates of Mercy

Gypsies skilled me in telling the future
but I did not foresee this fate for me.
I fed to the poxy Perigos white mercury salts
in honeyed pudding, for cure not murder.
All know me, a cunning woman with recipes
and remedies, potions against possessions.
It will not do; famed throughout this town,
yet twelve gawping men see only sorceress
or slut. They huddle quick, bestow the gallows;
the gates of mercy close, wreathed in shadows.

3: Mary Bateman's Lament

Child, this day, as you sleep, I will hang.
I pleaded my belly to escape the scaffold
until a crone jury poked that to a lie.
I am to die; there can be no charm in that.
The Ordinary prevails on me to confess,
that compassion not given here may be found
beyond the grave. I will not trick any more.
No poisoner, but a thief whom no angel will save
from the drop when I must dance as a demon.
Remember me, daughter, a mere striving woman.

Notes from the Beggar's Benison

1737, St. Andrew's Day. Twenty-four met,
three tested and enrolled; all frigged.

A good day then for the most puissant order:
two hospitable posture molls most intimately

surveyed – the delights of foreign countries
laid bare, no shifts nor smallclothes to veil

mysterious estuaries or shores. Merryland
well discovered and plowed; no opportunity

lost for us cock-mongers. Most edifying.
Thomas stiff as a three-penny upright,

tallywags alert to every prospect of the test,
we all pull together and the platter is full.

Three on the prick glass are confounded;
Fanny Hill is read; all broken up at 3 a.m.

A convivial celebration. Nothing fails us, who
as lord, judge and parson go to slumber;

strengthened for a new day, when all damnable
doctrines or immoral impieties will be scotched.

Gentlemen, this evening's doings let us well recall;
drain the bumper, snuff the candle, God bless us all.

Jorvik Afternoon

In the cupcake café coffee-steam tendrils rise from the bowl,
like a tree of life bridging to heaven.

On the next table, around a well of rain, three women sit,
casting knowing looks over cell phones,

splayed like carved runes. They spin out stories; a word web
capturing all that has happened,

all that might come to be. One grins knowingly for a selfie;
a click freezes her in a place already behind her,

telling only of what's past. The next totes an Ann Summers bag.
"It's a present", she laughs, "for a close friend."

The third flicks cigarette ash, "tomorrow may not come"
tattooed up her arm. Her yellow t-shirt

says "yellow is not my colour," begging the question.
Maybe the one they should ask me:

am I losing the thread? Nothing is as it seems. All is interim
echoes a gargoyle in the Minster stoneyard.

His destiny is for higher things; he chides us who unspool
quietly in the breeze, who spout nonsense below.

Her Mother's Fur Coat

"the end of the affair is always death"
ANNE SEXTON

It wasn't that cold
for October
in Massachusetts
but enough chill
to make
her mother's fur coat
a rational choice

fifteen years hanging
in the labyrinth
darkness of the closet
it rose
to the occasion
arms hung out
a dusty red embrace

you offer yourself to
Asterion
soused with vodka
old perfume reek
roaring
for the garage
where the obedient car

at one turn of the key
surged current
ignited   the monster

V8 rumbles   chthonic
falls back
to a muted murmured chant
from the pit

the front seat   a woman
regresses
into   a fur coat
ringless   to complete
a deeper circle   head down
the engine   will stop
the worn satin lining   cool.

To Miss Jessica Rowland-Jones

*(on buying, in an Oxfam bookshop, her
Dannie Abse collection)*

Did you get that degree?
I expect so but, more,
I hope you savoured
the poems, so considerately
dissected in a prim, sober
undergraduate's hand.

Annotated, in black and red
mark you, as if you clocked on
for a later shift, unsure
if all possibility for profit
was trawled or shoals might
skulk still under deeper waters.

Though helpful to see that
change is a regular occurrence,
to know *history won't go away*,
it is those poems you ditched,
flouted in their mute iceberg dignity,
that leave me helplessly drunk.

Those where the singing voice,
from Ogmore keened, sharp-edged;
a *cyhyraeth* that could shudder
a spine easier than Tusker Rock
might splinter an unwary keel;
well left, Miss Rowland-Jones, well left.

Ergo Sum

These JYA girls pulse like shining
platelets, through backstreet San Polo;
scouring calle or canal, clumping

in churches and galleries, eager to
ensure everything sticks. Voices trill
like burnished castrati, fluting up

columns and altars in search
of the awesome; the point, click, flash
epiphany of being there.

Maybe more opera buffa than serious
work; though, at sunset, as a vaporetto
sluices past San Marco, elevating iPads

and iPhones, the girls become as numinous
as Tintoretto cherubs, concelebrants
of the mystery of the eternal digital now.

The Stone Pickers

*(A conversation with The Stone Pickers by Sir
George Clausen, Laing Art Gallery, Newcastle)*

If you were a stone picker,
that look of resigned surprise
at the pile of stones, defying gravity
to bubble up from the meadow around
your carefully scuffed boots,
would become you.
As it is that pail (water? milk?),
that artfully propped basket
(the almost gingham cloth
draped studio-careless across it),
that washed-out high-buttoned
sexless dress, world-weary
incline of shoulder
are, no less than you, mere artifice
Though, Polly (may I call you that?)
I may be too flinty with you.
Nursemaid, haymaker,
shepherdess, village girl –
you worked in fields, stood at gates
offered up head, shoulders, body
to the filleting and resolving gaze –
whatever the master ordered up,
you would become.
No less than the painter though,
I can fabricate a narrative of you;
it would speak of subversion.
How that whippet-tense body

would clamp, obdurate
at the raising of the brush.
How you fingered that
swaddle-tight, hessian apron-
almost empire line under your breasts -
as if it was the swirl of a ball gown
and you were celebrating
a full dance card.

You understood well
that woman/servant ju-jitsu
which rendered flexible
the painter's hold on you.

The Respectable Working Class

Week in, week out, I give my labour for
next to nowt. I've doffed my cap threadbare;
tugged my forelock so fierce
my hairline recedes from the back.

I've seemed grateful for mistress's
sawdust buns, for master's leaking roof
above my head, where I wake
each sun-up, practicing my yokel grin.

Come Sunday they want much more;
want me to deny my own self. I draw
the line at that. Aye, I'll go, sit in the pew,
bide quiet, think "more pigs, less parsons."

I pull the curtains across the window
of my soul. I become opaque.
They prate on about heaven's rewards
while I think of Jenny warm under the down;

afterwards, buttered toast, scalding
sugared tea, the smell of her on my skin.
I hear the choir sing – *The rich man
in his castle, the poor man at his gate.*

Amen, I'll say, and look pious too, but
mark this, and mark it well, when the time
of tribulation comes, the first will surely
be last and well on their way to Hell.

St. Christopher House

("potential Company HQ building to let; may sell")

Set among an epidemic of the same,
an anonymous brick and glass corporate
box that once sequestered hope, squats
empty and bereft. All burdens of buying
and selling it once carried, floated away
in the river run of recession.
Nothing to lose your head about;
it sinks, without grace, into a pelmet
of buddleia, ragwort and sedge.

Through vertical blinds, sun stripes
a vacant office; it is a reliquary
where the holy relics are:
palm prints smudging glass doors
like feathery smears on Easter icons;
greasy fingerprints around an intercom
agnostic about the possibility of response;
a telephone handset adrift on the floor,
whose reverential hum is a forlorn prayer.

Too often I have left similar rooms, void
as an emptied jar; locked doors, leaving
only an absence enclosed, as in a church
after a funeral, when parting
is despairing and expectant both.

A Scenic Life

This is the slow
haul up the ratcheted rail.

The cabled lift
hums like a congregation

that has almost
forgotten familiar words;

the car clunks
on towards the present

equipoise where
the broader prospect

is discovered.
Look behind – the start

of the excursion
too handy by half. Look

ahead – the steepest
decline foreshortens,

the end of the ride
palpable now.

Car and passenger
railroaded

on a gravity ride, held
at tipping point

where, unbalanced,
the careering

fall into the dark tunnel
mouth is all.

Vanitas

You would think it started with a photograph,
maybe black and white, certainly dog-eared;
but it didn't. So I am able to tell this as I wish.
It was me and Phil – mid '60s – on Friar's Point
where I stand now, watching a metallic sea
scraping a thin white scar along the beach.
I think The Small Faces were Number One
but it could have been The Kinks.
It was summer, more than likely sunny;
a lazy Sunday afternoon? Lazing on a sunny
afternoon? Depends on what was Top
of the Pops I guess. An old man stopped –
I say "old" but he was maybe younger
than I am now. He was old enough though –
a talking skull. Not cutting edge like us –
we were late Mod – back-combed, Ben
Sherman-ed; just before Hippy got me,
electrical engineering got Phil.
"I was born here lads" said the old man,
"but haven't been back for years.
I loved this place; take this view, it's all
that kept me going sometimes. Look at the wild
flowers – dying back now but they'll return
next Spring. It's good to be here; nowhere else
in the world holds a candle to it."
Maybe we said "fab" but probably not,
as it would've been a little uncool even then.
Perhaps, embarrassed, we searched for a reason
to walk but held by the Grammar School-boy
politeness to elders, we stayed put, piniond
to his story, which did involve a lot of bad luck,

though I'm short on detail as I didn't listen
too hard and don't want to make it up now.
Anyhow, he stopped going on, asked the time,
wandered off somewhere. I guess at most,
we would have said "weird" or something,
(not "awesome" which is too contemporary
for this poem). Whatever, it would have meant
 "you are not of the same universe as us.
What knowledge have you to share?
Our life is immanent, process and eternal.
We'll carry forever this Sunday, the endless
possibility of being sixteen, the inevitability
of check hipsters, the ability to sing obscure
soul music, (the black boys on the fairground
rides turning their heads in amused approval),
I think the old man would've liked
Frank Sinatra, or maybe Matt Monro
if he thought himself cool – it's difficult to tell
on such short acquaintance. Anyway,
now I'm here, on the spot where it all happened
forty odd years ago; dragging on this memory
like it was the last cigarette in the world.
Looking around for someone to confess to
that I'm leaving this town for the last time;
hoping for epiphany to cross the blood brain
barrier and bring enlightenment. My Spanish
cigarette pack warns of "una muerte lenta
y dolorosa" if I continue to smoke them.
Alone on Friar's Point, it is hard to imagine
that there could be any other kind.

The Immortal Game

1: Opening gambit

Dot plays a Spanish game
on the black and white patio;
her pieces circled
in a last stand for fun.
There'll be Ken and Mags,
Trish and Stan,
Les, Judith and John.
Each new arrival
to the set bigged up:
…remember when…
…I could have…
and then we...
she nearly…
An army of occupation
bivouacked for a week
at the Hotel Costa Calero.

2: Middlegame

Rosaria stretches across
the warm sheets
smoothing them flat,
feels the moonlit bay
at Hondagua lap cool
through her fingers;
arranges soap and shampoo
on a glass shelf,
sees her mother placing santos
on the home altar.
Rosaria genuflects
to pick up towels
from the bathroom floor,
sees La Naval rise golden
above the peasants,
squeezes her daughter's hand.
She fingers her beads,
feels the notes folded
in her pocket
itch against her thigh.
She swabs the floor,
the smell of bleach reassuring
in its tart emptiness,
its absence of promise
or consequence.

3: Endgame

Terry on the balcony –
black shirt, black slacks –
stands like a charioteer,
stretches each hiking sock,
heel and toe, pegs them
to a nifty plastic dryer.
He cranes his neck,
looks down
on the citronella glimmer,
hears the gintonic clamour;
clocks Dot queening it below,
(where's Terry-boy
when you need him?)
bangles and beads,
bright and shiny,
skirt like a valance
under an unmade bed

Terry winks at the maid,
will leave her a good tip,
but for now
blows her a kiss off his fingers
and joins the party
to castle Dot's king.

The Governor's Bath-House, Sydney

"we know not the builder nor his son"
W. H. AUDEN

The governor's bath-house is not there;

                a few cubes of stone
stand still, the rest crated and carted
by command to a new project. A tour guide
slips me a story about governors – Bligh,
Brisbane, Macquarie, Darling – I can walk
their streets, drink in their bars, but see
instead the mason's initials chiselled neat
on the stone face left behind.

                At the *Hero of Waterloo*
rub a finger over a shamrock, a careful
"TM" cut below – the sandstone yielding
to the tool as a lover to an embrace;
graffito of a craftsman transported,
repossessing his self in shameless lavish
of his time.

                Take the black candlestick
in the museum – convict's section – mere
turnings, shards of metal wrought, twisted,
compelled to become something degraded
scrap had no right to be – a carrier of light.

The governor's bath-house is not there.

Café Caryatids

In the Café Caryatids
an old man rests,
blue painted chair
tilted in the doorway.
He sat there yesterday,
will be there tomorrow.
Teeth and pullover holed
and brown, he stares
mute at the road, where
a drone of tourists pass.

Bacchants and satyrs
they follow the umbrella
thyrsus, snake through
café chairs and shop-fronts,
short-stepping in rhythm
after a guide. Yellow tights,
black ankle boots, she is
a queen, finding euro honey
in the columns and slabs
littering Apollo's temple.

Its residue, a carved
trilithon, faces westwards,
leads nowhere now,
admits to nothing.
At sunset, a lizard's eye
unblinking red,
on which shutters click,
cameras flash; the moment
when light folds into darkness
always elusive.

The Ladies of Doña Sofía

One by one the ladies of Doña Sofía
hatch from shuttered sleep, look up,
smell the spent storm, red with sunrise
and African dust, move its rucksack
of cloud, towards the Sierra Bermeja.

Out they come, tentative, like pupae
unspun prematurely from cocoons,
each touched gently by the sun moving
across the apartment block face.
Sessile dolls suddenly wrenched

free, their limbs rejoicing, they clean.
This is a synchronous choreography;
a *bulerias* where all hear the rhythm,
know the steps, feel the beat; all hold
the seed of sorrow close to their heart.

Each one cloths a window's damp smear,
as if waving desperate goodbye
to a lover, until a pin sharp reflection
emerges, like a magic painting,
in which each, in sequence, sees blue sky,

apartment blocks, ladies cleaning windows.
Tonight these imagos will metamorphose
their drab for Mass; imagine sins to commit,
finger beads for Our Lady of the Rosary,
scrub clean their shadowed souls.

Seamus and Paddy Build a Dam

Paddy shuffles up,
sign this for me,
holding out a pay packet receipt;
another week wrestling
the pneumatic drill,
bouncing off the reservoir floor
for two pence an hour more.

What will I write?
*Put Pa, sure they'll know who
dat is; t'will be grand.*

You're all thick paddies,
the ganger passing by.
Seamus looking on, stands
a big square Mr Strong;
tipping his brown envelope into
his hand, notes and coins
counted out, delicate
pearls against the calloused palm:

*some for the lassies,
some for the bhoys,
some for Mary in Macroom*

August 1971,
their homecoming aborted.
New Burtons, spit shined brogues,
hair oiled slick –
hearing the news from Belfast

in a bar near the port;
waking up penniless in Fishguard.
Hitching back to the building site
to ride the compressed air;
under pressure, rock faced,
grinding the point to the wall.

In the bar tonight
they'll sing rebel songs,
nurse grievance, right wrongs.
Pray Jesus, Mary and the holy Guinness,
down their pints, order more.
Quote Yeats, Kinsella, Kavanagh.
Sing out too loud,
here's one for McAdorey
the brave volunteer.

Seamus and Paddy,
two black and white men-
like sharecroppers in a photograph -
stripped bare to the waist,
bandanas tied to necks,
backs always bent, grinning
in the jackhammer's *totentanz*...

let us now praise famous men.

The Prof

I dreamed of running wild on urban drags,
through two-stroke testosterone nights,
with a motorbike gang. I dreamed of knowing
crank cases, dry clutches, 0 – 60 times;
putting down Hamlet,
picking up Haynes,
sliding into scratchy one-piece leathers,
oily quiff, oily hands,
the faint smell of burned rubber
trailing behind me.
They would nickname me "the Prof" –
my syntax as slick as an automatic
gear change;
my references as manifold
as the boys on a run;
my accent farther back
than the police on the bypass.
I would be tolerated as harmless,
a mascot, a good luck
token for the ton-up boys;
mothered by the girls astride –
pillioned, plump and leathered
like old coffee bar banquettes.
One day I would come into my own:
some knowledge suddenly needed,
a quick reaction to a dangerous situation –
reluctantly shouldering a hero's responsibility
would save the day,
but cost my life
on a tight bend, a wet road, a dark night.

But firmly in the pantheon of biker gods,
forever spoken off in hushed tones
seen coming fast through the pack,
90…95…100…
the Prof will always ride on.

I want a motorbike, I'd tell my Mum,
a Dominator;
over my dead body she'd reply.
I didn't care,
I was always a Mod anyway.

Kite

Newspaper, scissors, twine
culled from scullery, twigs
from estate birches – a soviet
of children builds a wing
under a still, lowering sky.

Too young to run far from the past,
they race fast forward yanking
the string, hoping for lift. It won't fly,
and a boy will not run again
except in dreams of kites.

A Simple Game

for Mary Baker

Chopping fruit for an
Autumn dessert,
the rhythm of knife
on wood board lulls me.

I see my mother,
pinnied, in a 50s
formica kitchen
peeling a Bramley.

It was a simple game:
each scrape of peeler
released an inch
of shiny spiral,

until a double helix
dangled unbroken,
flexing like a snake
on a blackthorn branch.

She gave me the knife:
if I could do it, tease
out my own green spring,
the blade would halve

a white apple heart
to be dipped in demerara;
always, like this memory,
tasting bitter sweet.

Sure of Father: VE Day, 2015

What brings you to mind
is not the celebration
of a remembered war.
It is a late-night film,
Private Buckaroo (1942).
The Andrews Sisters –
aglow with tempera smiles,
razor-sharp WAC uniforms,
pageboy rolls – tug
onstage a model tree.
Harry James' trumpet wails,
the band swings,
the girls finger pop, sing out
Don't Sit Under The Apple Tree.

I bought you *The Very Best Of…*
When the house was cleared
it was on the bookshelf, cellophaned.
Like the war, you became history,
chose not to speak for yourself,
resisted – kept mum.
In the space I make a simulacrum;
a daydreamed man,
who liked American swing
who drove bren-gun carriers
who hit a cricket ball out of Europe
who guarded other people's palaces
who, for fifty years, gracefully
watched an apple fall close and root.

Alphabet Baby

White T-shirt and blue denim trousers flat and bloodied
on the TV screen; on these cold clothes white circles
appear like the progression of a new disease. I think
of advertisements, a miracle powder to remove this stain.

I am learning to creep backwards downstairs

You could not speak the words for pain or despair
yet you knew them. The language you acquired was
inarticulate; it slithered towards you embracing
a vocabulary of kick, hit, throw, punch.

I am beginning to understand the meaning of "now"

A hologram of a child, your face bleached in a cauldron
of hate; skin white, tight across the bone; eyes sewn shut
with a thread of tears. Imagine a different world,
before the womb that carried you to this place of skulls.

I like to run but I fall or bump into things sometimes

Alphabet baby in shadow-lands between Alpha and Omega;
shorthand for a forsaken child, you come and go only
as anonymous victim. There is talk of lessons learned
but we make space by unlearning earlier, better ones.

Your death has been an education;
I have learned that chocolate hides bruises.

Bartimaeus Sees His Way Clear

It wasn't at all the worst pitch
though, all was, as always, black.
OK, so I would never be rich,
but those that walked the track

from town salved their guilt, a coin
dropped onto my spread cloak,
enough to keep me alive. The *soigne*
passers-by always saw me as a joke –

the blind beggar laid in the dust
forever ready with a toothy grin;
but under my breath I cussed
them all and their pious chagrin.

Worse, I cursed the puppeteer
who tied, then cut my strings,
left me squatting in the dust here,
with only prayers rising on wings.

To my father, to see was to know,
in which case he must think me thick.
There's little in this darkness to crow
about; reduced to this pathetic shtick.

But I think I know a faker when I see one;
take this preacher, the messianic Jew,
pretending to be the favoured son,
more empty promises, more ballyhoo.

It all looked suspicious to me but
this, after all, is god-bothering Jericho;
what was lost in humouring the mutt,
this fantasy messiah, a real holy joe.

"Son of David, have mercy on me,"
I called out and caught his attention –
flatter them, a golden rule for the payee,
the only way to build up your pension.

So many in the crowd that day
I had to shout; not expecting much,
maybe a few *lepta* tossed my way
from the purse of the godly nonesuch.

I wasn't converted, despite the aura,
but they lifted me from coin and cloak,
carried me to this rewriter of the Torah.
I'm blind not deaf but when he spoke

my ears didn't work, I "heard" inside –
sounds very strange but it's gospel true.
To the query, *what do you want?* I replied
That's easy, mate – a whole new world-view.

Your faith has cured all your ills
he said, and it's true I suddenly saw the lot
clear down to Jerusalem's olive hills,
the crowd near me yelling like zealots.

Then it struck me; I was out of a job.
I couldn't see myself in any skilled work;
all I knew was sucking up to the mob,
eating dust and playing the poor jerk.

Well, he would have to see me right,
it was his fault I was unemployed.
I hadn't asked for some white knight
to blunder in, leave my future destroyed.

But eyeing him, he seemed transparent –
a blinding light pouring from feet, hands,
side – beaming away as if some heir apparent,
not a drifter in these desolate badlands.

He held out a hand, pointed to Jerusalem
as if inviting me to travel to the holy town.
No chance! It was soon Passover, all confusion;
the Romans not fussy whom they cut down.

Though I believe myself a man of honour –
and I could see he had done me proud –
time to *be'shu'shu*, him looking every inch a goner.
Head down, I vanished from sight in the crowd.

Trio for Roy

i.m. Roy Bickford Jackson

1

We are large and loud, compensatory in our arrival
on the ward; ambassadors from a world
with which there are no diplomatic relations.
We are levelled, our dark outside smell overwhelmed,
our geniality dissolved.

You lay propped like a pasha in a four-bed ward,
the more easily to be grabbed, wheeled, pumped, manoeuvred.
whatever it is they will do to keep life going.

We have lost you to this place now;
the ward owns you; we won't get you back.
You are theirs – these nurses and doctors,
with their routines, interventions,
their rigorous kindliness, brisk competence.

Tubes, readouts, dials, wipes, respirators,
all smile on your dying; us and them are conspirators,
ignoring the truth we all acknowledge but don't speak.
In this ultra bright room nothing can be hidden;
we are only moving through, you will stay.

2

Now, from this bed,
extremity has lightened you
cut you loose to move easily
between times and places.
Kindly, you involve us in the stories
you have been wanting to share.

...in a brothel in Cairo,
we couldn't find the women...
when we stopped we would,
in this order mind,
dig a slit trench
bury petrol cans
bury bully beef;
it was done for safety
and a stash for on the way back.
we had potatoes
but the petrol had evaporated
so we put sand in the tin
and lit it;
we roasted the spuds and the beef
and thought Jerry could fuck himself
because we were warm and fed
we were alive in this chilling desert,
we had the trenches...
You going eh?
That'll put an end to your antics then...

We have a photograph of you in Alexandria –
in mufti, a café framed by palms
that a desert wind might be rustling.
With a friend and a full head of dark hair,
a pipe clenched, you read a newspaper;
secure in having come through so far
confident of the journey ahead.

You seemed happy in Egypt.
We could leave you there content
but for the dreams; you say
you are falling, must hold the bed tight.
You are falling out of this world.

3

Thirty-six years ago in this emptied room
I asked if I could marry your daughter;
waiting for a break in the cricket on television.
How will you support her? you asked between overs –
but you didn't say no.

Years of sunlight exploring through
the glass lean-to have fingered gently
the books; when we move them
there are book-shadows burned
onto the shelving like a valediction.
Panel pins tacked into the wall, now

hold down total eclipses where plates once hung.
Wallpapers – pink striped, yellow, embossed –
stand out; a carpet piece uncovered in a corner
shines too brightly in its original colours,
like a butterfly emerging in a winter garage.

I opened a window,
punched it hard,
the frame quivered;
green paint flakes,
faded matt, cracked off.
I did it for contact
with the cold air,
the life of streets,
visible but distorted
by the water on the panes
drawn out of the damp clothes
drying on the radiator.

I ironed them to dry them off,
the iron was old, a dead weight,
each pass released steam;
the cord was frayed and dangerous.
I made a note to repair it later.

You could wear these polo shirts
on holiday; on the beach
lying back in a deckchair comfortable
and content with friends.

I won't need to take them to the hospital today.

Clearing the house
we bring down a wardrobe;
I notice the neatness
of mortice and tenon joints;
the order implied by shelves labelled
"sundries," "shirts," "collars," "underwear."
We exaggerate the weight,
stepping over-carefully,
talking up the job
like two furniture removers on a contract.
Feet first, it groans down the stairs,
is cartwheeled through the front door into the garden.
It lands heavily.
Two doors hang open on the grass;
a bevelled mirror reflects
a depthless, empty blue sky
across which nothing moves.

I step carefully over broken wood,
close them,
finally.

C'an Freixa

A kingfisher flies out of the trees;
as complete as a telescope
closing in on itself with a snap,
it hits the window hard, drops.

In my hand it lies, gaudy,
useless as a lost evening purse.
It's the bird's absence I feel,
palpable; in the garden – where

goodbyes hung like condolences,
hugs were straitjacket embraces.
The empty air still holds the drag
of blue light, a rolling bolt of silk

like a neon ripple; a memory,
a slick feathering of the lemon
tree leaves, wet with sour rain,
dropping like tears down a pietà.

You drove from C'an Freixa,
looking in your wing mirrors;
the ones that say, careful, objects
might be nearer than they appear.

Notes

Mauerfall
Literally "wall fall" – the colloquial German expression for the fall of the Berlin Wall.

Shenanigans
In June 2014 BBC Leeds news reported that a fox was nightly stealing mens' shoes in a Leeds suburb and dumping them outside a woman's house. "Shenanigans" is thought to derive from the Irish (*sionnachuighim*) for playing the fox or fool.

Yiannis In His Bar
The Kontakion is a part of the burial service in the Orthodox tradition – "with the saints give rest, O Christ, to the soul of Thy servant where there is neither sickness, nor sorrow, nor sighing, but life everlasting." Bones are washed in wine before being moved from the grave to an ossuary.

Mary Bateman's Lament
Mary Bateman, the so-called Yorkshire Witch who lived in Leeds, was hung in 1809 for murdering Rebecca Perigo by poisoning. She had led a life of petty theft and con tricks – one of which was a hoax involving a hen predicting the end of the world by re-laying eggs on which Bateman had written prophecies, a stunt that the credulous paid a penny to see. Her body was publicly "anatomized" in Leeds and strips of her skin were sold to the audience as charms. Her skeleton was only recently removed from display.

The Beggar's Benison
An eighteenth-century aristocratic gentleman's club in Scotland whose rituals celebrated male sexuality.

Her Mother's Fur Coat
Asterion is a Cretan name for the Minotaur.

To Miss Jessica Rowland-Jones
The *cyhyraeth* is a ghostly spirit in Welsh mythology, a disembodied moaning voice that sounds before a person's death. Legends associate the *cyhyraeth* with the coast of Glamorganshire where it is heard before a shipwreck.

Ergo Sum
JYA stands for Junior Year Abroad – an American undergraduate programme of cultural exchange.

The Stone Pickers
The main figure in this painting was not really a stone picker at all, but the artist's long-term model and nursemaid to the Clausen children. She was Mary Baldwin, known to the family as Polly. Clausen arranged for her to pose for at least seven paintings, in the guise of a shepherdess, a haymaker a village girl, and so on.

Vanitas
A category of painting especially associated with 16th- and 17th-century still-life paintings in Flanders and the Netherlands. Paintings executed in this style were meant to remind viewers of the transience of life, the futility of pleasure, and the certainty of death. They focused on images of the impermanent and fleeting.

The Immortal Game
A chess game played by Adolf Anderssen and Lionel Kieseritzky in 1851, acclaimed as an excellent demonstration of the romantic style of 19th-century chess play.

Alphabet Baby
Phrases in italics taken from *A Guide to the Growing Child*.

Bartimaeus Sees His Way Clear
Be'shu'shu is Hebrew slang for doing something quietly or secretively, behind the scenes, or without making a fuss about it.